For author Lisa Bunker and radical copyeditor Alex Kapitan,
providers of essential guidance and words of wisdom —L.R.

To Ms. Sabatacakis, my eighth-grade history teacher,
who facilitated my first deep dives into the past —L.S.B.

Text copyright © 2020 by Lisa Robinson
Jacket art and interior illustrations copyright © 2020 by Lauren Simkin Berke

All rights reserved. Published in the United States by Schwartz & Wade Books,
an imprint of Random House Children's Books, a division of Penguin Random House LLC, New York.

Schwartz & Wade Books and the colophon are trademarks of Penguin Random House LLC.

Visit us on the Web! rhcbooks.com

Educators and librarians, for a variety of teaching tools, visit us at RHTeachersLibrarians.com

Library of Congress Cataloging-in-Publication Data
Names: Robinson, Lisa, author. | Berke, Lauren Simkin, illustrator.
Title: Were I not a girl: the inspiring and true story of Dr. James Barry / by Lisa Robinson; illustrated by Lauren Simkin Berke.
Description: First edition. | New York: Schwartz & Wade Books, [2020] | Includes bibliographical references. | Audience: Ages 4–8. | Audience: Grades K–1.
Summary: "A picture book biography that tells the story of Dr. James Barry, born female, who lived as a man from age 18 to his death"—Provided by publisher.
Identifiers: LCCN 2019043191 | ISBN 978-1-9848-4905-2 (hardcover) | ISBN 978-1-9848-4906-9 (library binding) | ISBN 978-1-9848-4907-6 (ebook)
Subjects: LCSH: Barry, James, 1795–1865—Juvenile literature. | Women physicians—England—Biography—Juvenile literature.
Surgeons—Great Britain—Biography—Juvenile literature. | Male impersonators—England—Biography—Juvenile literature.
Classification: LCC R154.B324 R63 2020 | DDC 610/.92 [B]—dc23

The text of this book is set in Baskerville STD.
The illustrations were rendered in pencil, watercolor, and ink and assembled digitally.
Pencil appearing in color was drawn with HB pencil and colored digitally.
Book design by Rachael Cole

MANUFACTURED IN CHINA
2 4 6 8 10 9 7 5 3 1
First Edition

SELECTED BIBLIOGRAPHY

"A Female Medical Combatant." *Timaru Herald,* November 25, 1865. https://paperspast.natlib.govt.nz/newspapers/THD18651125.2.19.

Dronfield, Jeremy, and Michael du Preez. *Dr. James Barry: A Woman Ahead of Her Time.* London: Oneworld Publications, 2016. Kindle.

Hurwitz, Brian, and Ruth Richardson. "Inspector General James Barry MD: putting the woman in her place." *BMJ* (Clinical research ed.). February 4, 1989; 298: 299–305. ncbi.nlm.nih.gov/pmc/articles/PMC1835606/pdf/bmj00217-0035.pdf.

Kubba, A. K., and M. Young. "The Life, Work and Gender of Dr. James Barry MD (1795–1865)." *Proceedings of the Royal College of Physicians Edinburgh.* 2001; 31:352–356. rcpe.ac.uk/sites/default/files/r_the_life.pdf.

Were I Not a Girl

The Inspiring and True Story
⇒ of ⇐
Dr. James Barry

WRITTEN BY

LISA ROBINSON

&

ILLUSTRATED BY

LAUREN SIMKIN BERKE

schwartz wade books · new york

Imagine living at a time when you couldn't be
the person you felt you were inside.
You couldn't be true to yourself.

This is a story about someone who refused to let that happen:
Dr. James Barry.

DR. JAMES BARRY

It wasn't until he died
that his story became known.

Although he'd been born Margaret Ann Bulkley,
he lived for more than fifty years as Dr. James Barry.

Why did Margaret become James?
She never said.
Nor did he.

Let me tell you a little more about what we do and don't know. . . .

Margaret Ann Bulkley was born in Cork, Ireland, sometime around 1789.
We can't be sure—
there is no official birth record.

When Margaret was growing up,
most girls weren't sent to school.
And so she stayed home
or worked at the family grocery store.

Women weren't supposed to own property or hold jobs
other than governess, maid, or factory worker.
And so even though Margaret had big dreams,
the future looked small.

In 1798, the people of Ireland rebelled against their British rulers.

Margaret admired the soldiers marching through town.

Were I not a girl, I would be a Soldier! she later wrote.

I must honestly confess I would prefer a sword to a musquet

& I should like a pair of Colours.

But women could not become soldiers.

When Margaret was sixteen,
her father lost his store and home,
then abandoned the family.
Hoping to find work, Margaret and her mother braved traveling to London
across the war-tossed Celtic Sea.

Margaret's uncle, James Barry, who had just died,

had left them money enough for food and lodging.

Margaret scoured newspaper ads

for work as a governess.

Alas, she lacked the required education.

One of her uncle's friends kindly agreed to teach her

French, history, arithmetic, geography, and writing.

Meanwhile, Margaret tended to the four-year-old son
of another family friend
and devoured the books in his library.
Especially the medical books.

On walks through the city,
Margaret often passed Middlesex Hospital,
where medical students hurried to and fro.

How she yearned to join them . . .
but women could not become doctors.

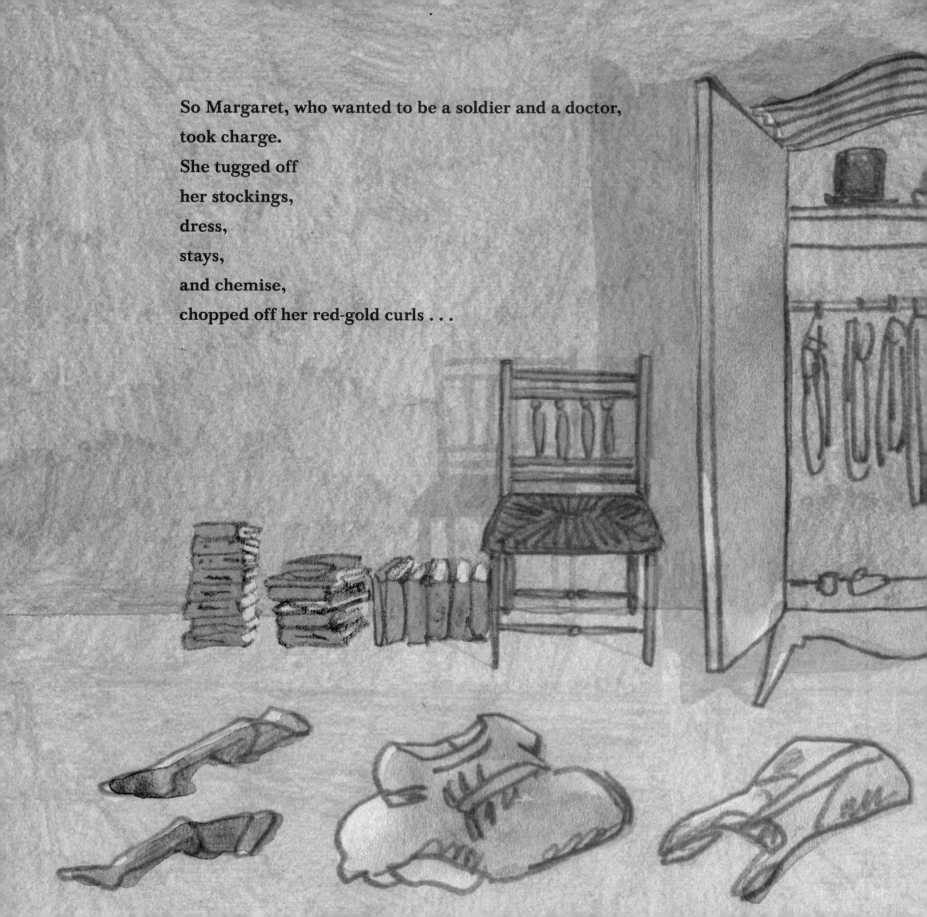

So Margaret, who wanted to be a soldier and a doctor,
took charge.
She tugged off
her stockings,
dress,
stays,
and chemise,
chopped off her red-gold curls . . .

and vanished.

In her place appeared a young man in
breeches,
a high-collared shirt,
a cravat,
and a tailcoat.
Choosing her uncle's name,
Margaret Bulkley became James Barry.

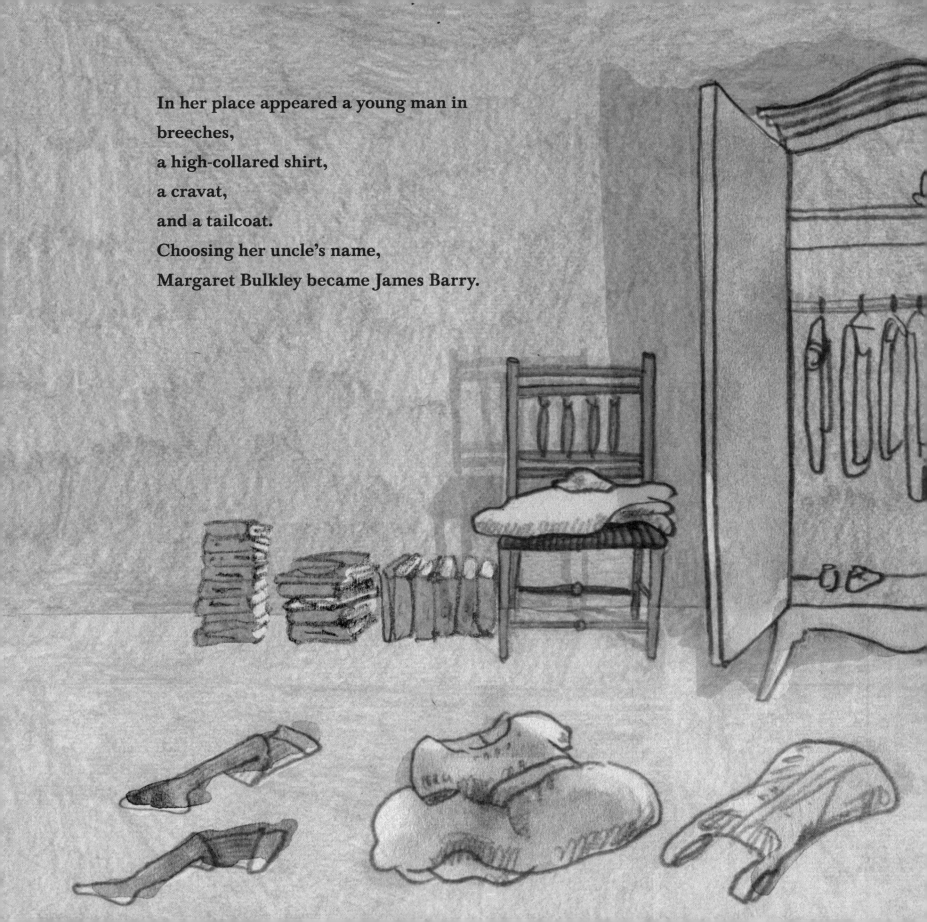

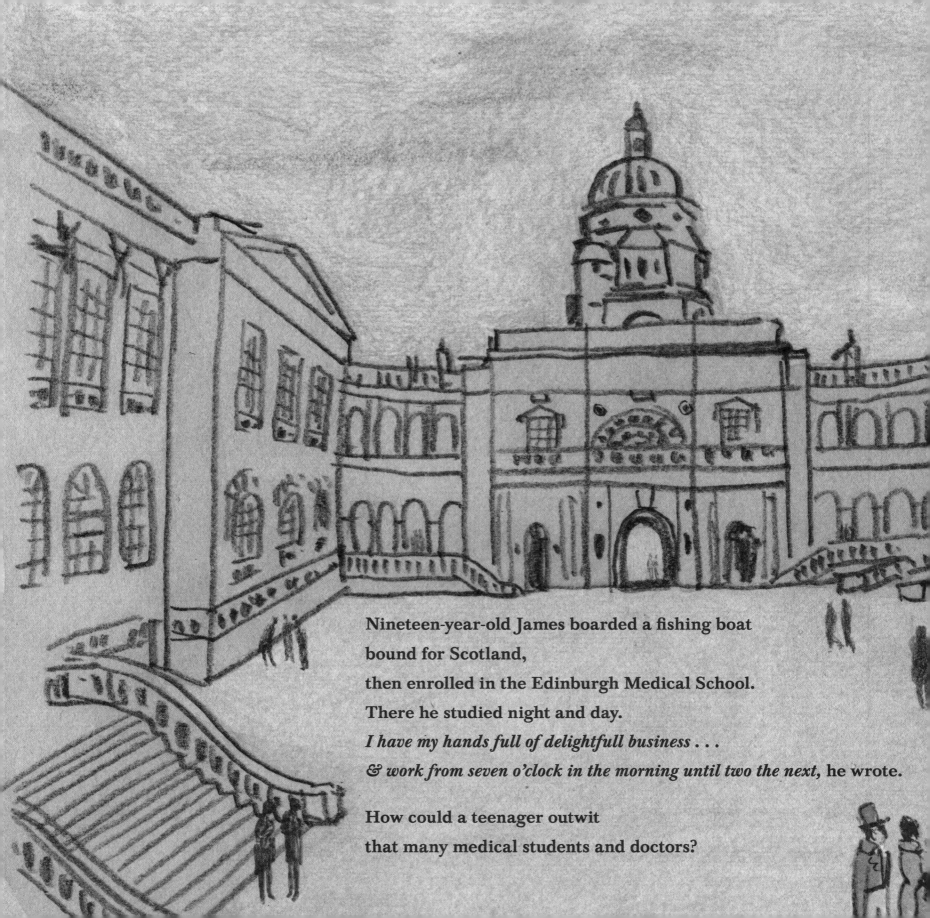

Nineteen-year-old James boarded a fishing boat
bound for Scotland,
then enrolled in the Edinburgh Medical School.
There he studied night and day.
I have my hands full of delightfull business . . .
& work from seven o'clock in the morning until two the next, he wrote.

How could a teenager outwit
that many medical students and doctors?

In truth, not everyone believed
that James belonged in medical school.
In his last year, the rumors began.
James's smooth skin, slight build, and high voice
led people to suspect that he was . . .

. . . a mere boy.
"Perhaps he's no older than twelve,"
whispered his fellow students.
The university declared him too young
to take the final exams essential to becoming a doctor.

Despite the university's decision,
James refused to give up.
Another family friend stepped in on his behalf.
There were no rules against boys
sitting for the required exams,
the friend argued.
And so the university senate allowed James
to take on the challenge.
He passed all the tests.
James was officially a doctor!

The young doctor moved to London for surgical training.

There he became quite a dandy.

He loved elegant fashion—
satin waistcoats,
lace cuffs and collars,
leather boots polished to a lustrous shine.

In 1813, he enlisted in the military.

Finally, James's dream of becoming a doctor and a soldier had come true.

How did he avoid being challenged?

Physical exams weren't required,

and His Majesty's forces really needed surgeons.

During his military service, James explored the world.
He sailed to South Africa, the West Indies, and St. Helena,
accompanied by a small menagerie.

Over the next fifty years,
James delivered babies,

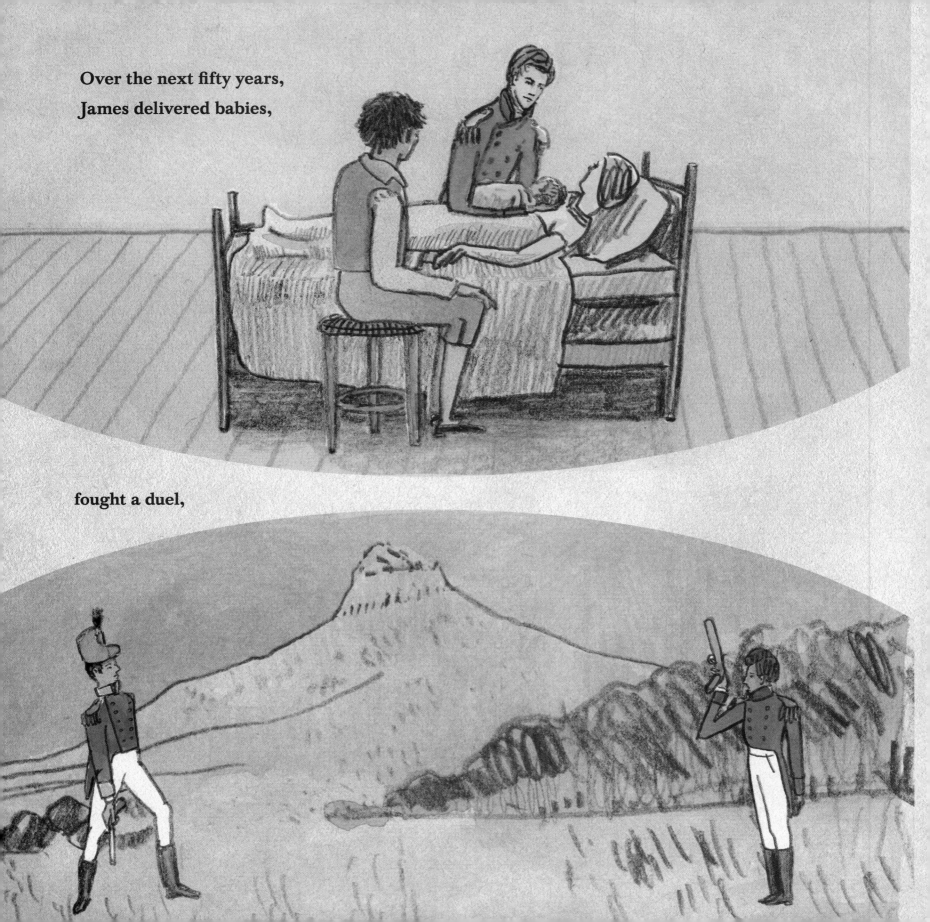

fought a duel,

fell in love,

and demanded clean water, fresh vegetables,
and proper medical care in prisons and hospitals.

In 1858, he was promoted to one of the highest military ranks—Inspector General of Hospitals.

James Barry died at the age of 76.
Or was it 70?

That's a question that will never be answered,
like many others about James's life.
Sometimes, no matter how hard we search,
answers remain hidden.

Still, one answer is clear:
James was living his truth.

MORE ABOUT DR. JAMES BARRY

Although James Barry's story leaves us with many unanswerable questions, there is a lot we do know about his life and achievements.

Who were the family friends who helped, and what did they know?

These patrons were all friends of Margaret's uncle, James Barry, a well-known artist. Dr. Edward Fryer tutored Margaret so she could work as a governess. General Don Francisco de Miranda, a Venezuelan revolutionary, offered her the use of his library. Lord Buchan helped James navigate medical school. There is no evidence that any of them knew that Margaret would become James or that James had once been Margaret. However, it is possible that they not only knew but also assisted with this plan.

Who did James fall in love with?

During his posting to South Africa, James fell in love with Lord Charles Somerset, the governor of the Cape of Good Hope. His feelings for Lord Somerset triggered an argument with a rival officer, Captain Cloete, resulting in a dramatic duel. Both men were injured but survived. It is not clear who won.

The close relationship between Dr. Barry and Lord Somerset provoked a scandal when they were accused of being lovers. At that time, a romantic relationship between two men was illegal; in addition, Lord Somerset was married. An investigation into the accusation produced no evidence of wrongdoing. They remained good friends until Lord Somerset's death in 1831.

What else did James accomplish?

James became a highly skilled surgeon who was a tireless advocate for access to health care for women, prisoners, lepers, and the poor. He stirred up conflict wherever he went, usually connected to his activism for hygiene in hospitals and better health care for the disadvantaged. In 1826, he performed the first documented caesarian section in which both the mother and the baby survived.

AUTHOR'S NOTE

Some people are born in a body that does not match who they feel they are on the inside. We now understand that gender—the term for how someone feels on the inside—is more than just male or female; it is a spectrum with a wide range of possibilities. Although Dr. Barry's family raised him as a girl, how he lived most of his adult life indicates that he likely identified as a man. Today the term *transgender* is used to describe a person who feels that their gender is different from the one they were assigned at birth.

There are many examples of women who lived as men at a time when openly changing one's gender was not accepted. Hannah Snell disguised herself as a man in order to serve in the British army for three years in the 1740s. In 1782, Deborah Sampson disguised herself as a man in order to fight for freedom with the Continental Army during the American Revolution. After their military service, both Snell and Sampson returned to living as women. Both cited patriotism and self-protection as reasons for what they did. But Dr. James Barry, who lived for over fifty years as a man, strived to maintain that identity throughout his life.

Today some people feel that traditional masculine and feminine pronouns like *he* and *she* do not fit their gender identity and prefer to use pronouns that are neutral and inclusive: *they* and *ze,* for example. If you are not sure which pronoun a person uses, you can ask them. For the purposes of this story, *she* was used for Dr. Barry's childhood, when he was known as Margaret Ann Bulkley, and *he* was used after he began living as James Barry.

ILLUSTRATOR'S NOTE

In creating my illustrations, I try to connect to both the experience and imagination of the reader. I do as much research as I can, then work to make the historical details seem effortless. In the case of Dr. James Barry, I was also able to draw upon my own life experiences. Rather than living as either a man or a woman, I identify as nonbinary, which means I get to be both and neither, allowing my gender to be based on how I express myself most naturally. Illustrating *Were I Not a Girl* was particularly meaningful to me because it highlights that transgender people have always existed and were able to figure out how to succeed on their own terms. I hope my portrayal of James helps readers feel they can be whoever they want to be, too.